Plan Your Wedding with Common Sense

JACLYN TOOPES

A Chicagoland Wedding Planner

ISBN: 1512394831
EAN: 978-1512394832

In loving memory of my grandparents, Eugene "Gene" and Therese Sullivan.

The love you shared through 65 years of marriage, the spunk you lived with, and the energy you brought to our family gatherings remain an inspiration for the entire Mahoney and Sullivan clan.

In true love story fashion, you left this world less than a month apart, but your spirit lives on in your children, grandchildren, and great-grandchildren.

I love you, Nana and Papa, and I hope that you don't mind me using your quotes throughout this book. They are, after all, quite phenomenal.

CONTENTS

A Message for the Bride and Groom

Hello there, beautiful bride and dashing groom-to-be. This book is entirely for you. Use it, learn from it, and refer to it. The sole purpose of the words on the pages that follow is to make your wedding planning experience enjoyable and as stress-free as humanly possible. So, if you're looking to grow closer together and to have fun, yes fun, while planning your big day, read on, my friends.

Cheers to a top-notch wedding planning experience and a wonderful life of laughter and love together! – Jaclyn Toopes

Introduction

Whenever you feel a twinge of stress about cake flavors, or worse, find yourself completely overwhelmed by cake flavors, I strongly encourage you to stop, take a deep breath, and remind yourself to use common sense. This simple little phrase will do wonders to clear your thoughts and help you focus on the basics of the task at hand.

Take those cake flavors you're freaking out about.

Assuming you're serving alcohol at your reception (which you should, unless of course you have religious or other reasons not to), at least half of your guests (more like 90% if you're Irish like me) will be partaking in your signature martini and other libations throughout the night. Are your tipsy friends and relatives really going to care about what your cake tastes like? Are they going to scoff at you for choosing carrot instead of white? Ummm, no. Realistically, *maybe* 60% of your guests will even take a bite of your cake, and those who are three-plus glasses of chardonnay deep (aka most of them) will have the munchies and devour whatever you toss their way at the end of the night. It's no secret that booze makes everything taste better.

Now, that's not to say that you should choose a totally crappy cake. But, unless you're a baker or cakes are your absolute *passion* (in which case you'll likely already know what you want and not be stressed about it), don't sweat whether to go with strawberry or chocolate filling. Pick something, check it off your list, and move on!

CHAPTER 1
COMMON SENSE ON VENDORS

Hire a wedding planner. Let's think about this. Do you want to save time? Do you want to save money? Do you want to feel like you're on cloud nine on your wedding day? Do you want your mom and your family (and your mom) and your friends (and your mom) to feel relaxed the month before your wedding (aka crunch time) and enjoy the experience with you? If your answer is yes to any of the above, do yourself and your loved ones a favor; hire a wedding planner.

Let's be honest: You wouldn't ask your kid brother to be your photographer. You wouldn't ask your uncle to be your DJ. And, it's safe to say that you definitely wouldn't ask your mom to give you an updo (at least I'd hope not). Realistically, you'd hire a professional photographer. You'd hire a professional DJ. And, of course, you'd hire a professional hair stylist.

So, should you put the pressure and stress on yourself and your loved ones to not only plan your entire wedding celebration, but to manage your big day and coordinate with all of the vendors you've hired? Hint, hint: The answer is no, you shouldn't.

I'm going to take a wild guess here and say that you've probably never planned a large-scale social event, let alone a wedding. A wedding planner has. This means that you get to bask in the expertise they bring to the table, the vendor relationships and deals they can offer you, the hours upon hours of research time and headaches they can save you. And, most importantly, you can rest assured knowing that a professional has your back throughout your planning process and on your wedding day.

This all equates to less stress and more fun for you! Who doesn't want that?! Not to mention, a wedding planner will provide creative and budgeting assistance in addition to vendor recommendations and proper etiquette guidance.

A venue coordinator is not the same as a wedding coordinator. I beg of you not to think that they are one in the same, because you will be sorely disappointed. Here's the difference: You are a wedding planner's #1 priority while a venue coordinator's #1 priority is the venue they work for.

A venue coordinator is exactly what their title implies. They coordinate the venue for events, including weddings. This may mean that they handle the organization of onsite catering, wait staff, table and chair set-up, and any specialized in-house décor requests. However, a venue coordinator doesn't handle all planning and day-of details or timeline and vendor coordination for the bride and groom.

A wedding coordinator, on the other hand, will guide you through the entire wedding planning process including negotiating service rates, reviewing contracts and selecting vendors, attending various appointments with you, coordinating with the venue coordinator and all vendors, and managing all details and logistics on your wedding day. Just think of your wedding planner as your longtime bestie throughout your planning processes.

Don't pick your vendors just because they're your friends. Even if your friend Tom is really into music and has what he calls "DJ equipment," that doesn't mean that he's a qualified wedding DJ who will be able to read the crowd and keep your dance floor bumping all night long.

Just like friends don't let friends drive drunk, friends don't let friends be their wedding vendors. That's not to say you can't hire your friends who are *professionals* in their line of work. But, people with hobbies or amateurs will most likely produce amateur services or work products. If you're willing to take that risk, then don't expect a professional product. Your best bet is not to chance it, and go with a pro. You can always tell your friend who offered their services that you'd rather they celebrated with you than worked on your wedding day. It's an easy out to avoid offending them.

Be leery of overly cheap services. If the sticker price is too good to be true, then the service is too good to be true too. That's just common sense. A city-based photographer who charges less than $1,000 for a full wedding day is likely either hurting for clients or an amateur with little experience. Just be sure you read reviews and even talk to past clients before booking a deal that seems like a steal. As the old adage goes, you get what you pay for!

Everything is negotiable. You email DJs; you call photographers; you meet with florists and caterers. They each lay out their package and pricing structure for you. Just remember, in the wedding industry prices are constantly fluctuating and nothing is set in stone. As a potential customer, you have a great deal of power when talking dollars and services with your wedding vendors.

Now, that's not to say that you should completely lowball the photographers you meet with. But, if you feel strongly that you need to stay within a certain budget for a specific area of your wedding, explain your reasoning to that potential vendor, and, more often then not, they will be willing to work with you. Don't be afraid to negotiate, because vendors may surprise you with what they're willing to offer within your price range. Remember, you'll never know unless you ask!

Book your vendors early. Don't get bogged down in researching and meeting with every vendor under the sun. Keep in mind that most vendors can only handle one wedding in a given weekend and once they're booked, you're SOL. So, while it's important to be choosy in picking your vendors, don't wait too long to pull the trigger. Venues, churches, photographers, and DJs often book their calendars up to a year or more in advance. So, if you find a vendor that you like, make sure to lock them down quickly before another savvy couple scoops them up.

Get everything in writing. And when I say everything, I mean *everything*. Contracts are ideal, but email acknowledgments or letters for smaller services are good too. The bottom line is that you don't want anything involving your wedding day to be a verbal contract. God forbid your limo doesn't show up on time to get you to the church because their receptionist wrote the wrong time in their calendar, or they send an 8-person ride instead of an 18-person stretch. Have fun cruising in your dad's beat-up truck to your ceremony (...awkward). Your contract with the limo company is your safety net and potentially a claim to compensation for these types of major mistakes.

This should go without saying, but make sure you thoroughly review all contracts, forms, and timelines with your vendors in detail. You don't want any surprises on your wedding day, like an additional service charge that wasn't discussed with you but is in your contract, or your venue using navy linens instead of silver because there was a typo in your contract and you missed it. Read and re-read your contracts before signing them. And, if you have a question about the details, don't be afraid to ask the vendor. Blindly signing something you're not sure about is a big no-no that could have some really negative consequences and cause major headaches or moments of panic for you down the road.

CHAPTER 2
COMMON SENSE ON BUDGETS

Set a budget. You're probably reading this saying, "Well, duh." And, you're right. This seems like the most obvious thing to do when planning a big, expensive event like your wedding. But, you'd be surprised at how many couples don't sit down and break down a budget before jumping into venue hunting, guest list drafting, and worse, spending! Early on, you and your fiancé should come to an agreement on how much you can personally spend on your wedding. A reasonable range is fine, but there shouldn't be more than a $10,000 difference in your low and high-end budget.

After establishing your personal budget, you should discuss with anyone wanting to help finance your wedding how much they can contribute and when. As awkward as you may think it is, if your parents are offering to help pay for all or part of your wedding, you need to talk to them about the amount they are contributing and at what point they can provide it. It's bad news bears to start planning and racking up expenses before you know how much you have to work with.

And remember, Microsoft Excel© is your friend when budgeting. You can break down your budget down into general categories including Ceremony, Reception, Décor, Music, Photography and Videography, Stationary, Wedding Rings, Transportation, Gifts, Bride, and Miscellaneous. Rank these categories in order of how much you think you'll spend in each, with 1 being the most expensive. You can then divvy up percentages of your budget for each area based on your rankings.

See the following example, Worksheet #1.

Anticipated Total Budget	$40,000.00

Planning Area	Ranking	Percentage
Ceremony	7	2%
Reception	1	50%
Décor	5	5%
Music	3	4%
Photography and Videography	2	10%
Stationary	9	3%
Wedding Rings	6	4%
Transportation	10	5%
Gifts	8	2%
Bride	4	10%
Miscellaneous	11	5%
		100%

You can then create a second worksheet that shows your suggested budget percentage for each category and suggested cost, Worksheet #2.

Planning Area	Your Suggested Percentage	Your Suggested Cost	Spent to Date
Ceremony	2.00%	$800.00	-
Reception	50.00%	$20,000.00	-
Décor	5.00%	$2,000.00	-
Music	4.00%	$1,600.00	-
Photography and Videography	10.00%	$4,000.00	-
Stationary	3.00%	$1,200.00	-
Wedding Rings	4.00%	$1,600.00	-
Transportation	5.00%	$2,000.00	-
Gifts	2.00%	$800.00	-
Bride	10.00%	$4,000.00	-
Miscellaneous	5.00%	$2,000.00	-
Totals	100.00%	$40,000.00	-
Planned Amount	$40,000.00		

Once you've ranked your budget categories (Worksheet #1) and configured your suggested percentages and suggested costs for each area (Worksheet #2), create a third worksheet to track your expenses. Whenever you have an expense, add that cost to Worksheet #2 in the Spent to Date column next to the appropriate budget category.

This allows you to compare your total budget for each particular budget area to what you have spent to date. See the examples on the following pages for Worksheet #3 and updates to Worksheet #2.

Date	Expenditure	Payee/ Vendor	Budget Category	Amount
1/12/15	Venue deposit	Venice Inn	Reception	$2,500.00
1/30/15	Photographer deposit	Lily Photos	Photography and Videography	$1,500.00
2/15/15	Wedding dress deposit	Bridal Bliss	Bride	$1,000.00
3/1/15	DJ deposit	M.J. DJs	Music	$1,000.00
3/3/15	Florist deposit	Blooms Inc.	Décor	$750.00
3/10/15	Videographer deposit	Tye Video	Photography and Videography	$500.00
3/12/15	Trolley deposit	Clark's Trolley Service	Transportation	$500.00
4/2/15	Veil	Bridal Bliss	Bride	$300.00

When you jump back to Worksheet #2, you can add each expense to your Spent to Date column. Now, you can see your expenses vs. your budget.

Planning Area	Your Suggested Percentage	Your Suggested Cost	Spent to Date
Ceremony	2.00%	$800.00	-
Reception	50.00%	$20,000.00	$2,500.00
Décor	5.00%	$2,000.00	$750.00
Music	4.00%	$1,600.00	$1,000.00
Photography and Videography	10.00%	$4,000.00	$2,000.00
Stationary	3.00%	$1,200.00	-
Wedding Rings	4.00%	$1,600.00	-
Transportation	5.00%	$2,000.00	$500.00
Gifts	2.00%	$800.00	-
Bride	10.00%	$4,000.00	$1,300.00
Miscellaneous	5.00%	$2,000.00	-
Totals	100.00%	$40,000.00	$8,050.00
Planned Amount	$40,000.00		

Stick to a budget. It may be super tempting to stretch your budget and spring for that extra upgrade to your bar package or order those baby blue chair covers that will cost $1,000 more than you planned to spend on décor. Keep in mind that you set a budget for a reason, and you want to avoid breaking the bank for your wedding.

A massive amount of wedding debt is not an ideal start to married life. So, don't second guess forgoing the chair covers and going with the standard bar. No one will notice the difference in your décor, and, trust me, your guests will be happy with whatever cocktails you serve.

"I'm a penny shy." – *Eugene Sullivan*

You can't have your cake and eat it too. Unless you're a multi-millionaire, you're going to have to prioritize where you spend your money. You may desperately want those $100 candelabras on all 20 tables at your reception, but is that really the best use of that $2,000? Likely not.

Think about what is important to you and your fiancé, and then spend your money there. You may have to make sacrifices and forgo the mini milkshakes at the end of the night if you'd rather have another appetizer option for your guests. Make decisions based on what's best for your personal budget, and don't look back.

Don't forget hidden costs like service charges, taxes, tips, and postage. Again, read and re-read your contracts, and remember to analyze the pricing structure and payment schedule in each of them. Oftentimes, caterers and venues in particular will have service charges and taxes that are in addition to the per person price they list in their packages. It's not uncommon for service charges to range from 15-25%, so make sure you're aware of how much that translates to in dollars.

It's also common courtesy to tip vendors like your officiant, ceremony musicians, limo driver, and hair and makeup artists. The only time it's really socially "optional" to tip such service providers is if they own their own company and all of your payments are going directly to them as opposed to the company owner or a corporation. Still, tips are always welcomed and appreciated by any of the above vendors.

Another charge that may creep up on you is postage. Don't let it! Stamps for save the dates, invitations, and thank you notes add up quickly. Always factor in postage costs, which you won't really know until you visit your local post office. Oddly shaped, large, or heavy invites will logically cost more. So, be aware of postage costs, and don't forget to factor those estimates into your budget at the outset of planning.

Don't bank on making money off of your wedding. You're not a psychic so you can't predict how much money your guests can and will offer as wedding gifts. So, don't try to guess. And please, please, please don't count on gift money to pay for any day-of wedding expenses. That may have been the norm 30 years ago in paying for your end of the night bar tab, but it's risky business in today's world, my friends.

"A day late and a dollar short." – Eugene Sullivan

CHAPTER 3
COMMON SENSE ON DECISION-MAKING
AND ORGANIZATION

Have a wedding planning timeline. Some people are natural procrastinators. While it may have gotten you through high school algebra, cramming won't cut it for planning your wedding. Even if all you have is a loose monthly schedule that gives you some direction and keeps you (and your loved ones) from pulling your hair out the month of your wedding when you realize you still haven't ordered a cake or finalized tux sizes for the groomsmen, it's better than nothing.

If you're lost on where to start and don't have the budget for a planner, that grand old thing called the Internet has a magical world of templates and schedules specific to wedding planning. Some are even downloadable and free! That's a win for you and definitely a good place to start customizing your personal wedding planning schedule.

Have a wedding weekend timeline. Lack of a schedule breads disorganization. Disorganization breads chaos. Chaos is the last thing you want on your wedding day, unless it's the last song of the night and everyone is getting down on the dance floor. That's pretty much the only case when wedding chaos is not only fun, but also entirely acceptable and encouraged.

If you haven't given people a timeline and clear, concise direction, it will be no one's fault but your own if your bridesmaids are half an hour late to their hair and makeup appointment or if your dad's speech goes 20 minutes longer than you've allotted. As tedious as it might seem, make scheduling arrangements in advance to get everyone on the same page. Your future self will thank you.

"I'm surrounded by assassins." – *Eugene Sullivan*

Get and stay organized. A Microsoft Excel© workbook is a great way to stay organized with your wedding planning timeline, wedding weekend timeline, budget and expenses, guest list, vendor list, and other various to do lists. Keeping a binder of all of your contracts and receipts or a folder on your computer is also a smart move.

You should also consider creating a wedding related email address using an email provider of your choice. For example, jmwedding@xxxxx.com. You will be inundated with emails from potential vendors, so it's a good idea to have a wedding related email box to keep yourself organized (and sane). However you decide to do it, keep everything wedding related in a centralized place.

Set parental boundaries. Some of us are daddy's girls or mama's boys, always have been, always will be. There's nothing wrong with that, except when you're planning your wedding with your fiancé. While it's great to enlist the help of your parents in planning parts of your wedding celebration, remember that you and your fiancé should be the ones making any final decisions. After all, it's a day to celebrate the two of you becoming your own little family, so it's important that you both have a say in your wedding day vision. When you feel a parent (or other relative or friend) is becoming overbearing in the planning process, again, keep in mind that final decisions should be made by you and your fiancé exclusively.

Go with your gut, no one else's. If you want to serve double-fudge brownies instead of traditional white-frosted cake, go for it! If you want to skip a bouquet and garter toss at your reception, go for it! If you want to serve a family-style meal instead of a plated one, go for it! The hope is that you're only doing this once, so give it your all and make it the day *you*, as a couple, want it to be.

Sure, you can listen to mom and dad's advice, especially if they're footing all or part of the bill. But, remember that it's your wedding, not theirs. If you feel pressured to blindly follow every little thing your parents (or whoever else is offering unsolicited options or their wallet) tell you to do, respectfully and pleasantly emphasizing that you've taken their thoughts into consideration (even if they're ridiculous or downright terrible) can help you break the news that you've gone a different direction without bruising egos. Hopefully, your parents have raised you to be independent, so show them what a good job they've done and stand your ground on those brownies!

DIY = Don't Invest Yourself. If you're not a creative person, you won't magically blossom into a florist, a carpenter, a designer, or an artist when planning your wedding. Don't kid yourself. Save yourself the time, money, and frustration of DIY projects by keeping them to a minimum.

You have enough going on when planning for your big day; don't add the unnecessary stress of carving, sanding, stenciling, and painting a custom

"Here Comes the Bride" sign. You can easily order that exact sign from countless stores online (and it will probably look better, no offense!). Even if you're tempted to learn calligraphy and address your own invitation envelopes, think about whether that's the best way to spend your precious time leading up to your wedding. DIY projects are often more time-consuming and costly than anticipated. What's that old saying? Oh yes, time is money. So, do yourself a favor and Don't Invest Yourself.

Delegate. It's 100% okay to ask for help. I repeat, it's 100% okay to ask for help. This even applies to you Type As like me. Remember, you're only one person and no one expects you to plan your entire wedding by yourself. Mothers and future mother-in-laws will likely be more than eager to help you with wedding tasks. Again, just make sure they know that you're running the show.

And, brides, don't forget to involve your groom. He's smart enough to marry you, so he's smart enough to take on some wedding planning responsibilities. A good task for him to take over is planning your honeymoon. He can also certainly manage planning transportation (i.e. limos and trolleys)

Even if you're leery of giving up control, challenge yourself to give it a try. You will be surprised at how much people, including your hubby-to-be, are willing to help and how much stress is lifted from your shoulders when you entrust others to check off some of those never-ending boxes on your wedding to-do list.

Keep your expectations of others in check.
No one can read your mind. Not your fiancé, not your mom, not your vendors, not your planner, and certainly not your guests. If you want something done a certain way, speak up. If you're getting married on the beach but want all of your guests in somewhat formal attire, you better tell them that on your invitation. Otherwise, don't be surprised when Uncle Joe shows up in cargo shorts, an obnoxious Hawaiian shirt, and his favorite bright blue flip-flops. Yikes!

Consider an off-season wedding. Busy season for the wedding industry is April through December. While this leaves a narrow window for the off-season, there are plenty of deals to find at top-notch venues if you're willing to tie the knot in January, February, or March. Not to mention, your bargaining power with vendors instantly increases with an off-season wedding. As noted earlier, everything is negotiable.

Send save the dates and invitations early. Get your date on your guests' calendars early. I'm not talking about a 2-year lead-time. That's a bit overboard. But, there's nothing wrong with sending a save the date 10-12 months in advance, especially if you're getting married during busy season (remember, that's April through December). Invitations should go out about 8-12 weeks before your wedding. If you're an eager beaver, there's no shame in sending them a tad earlier.

Don't get hung up on tradition. Again, it's *your* wedding, celebrating *your* love. People are there to support *you*. If you don't want to have a religious ceremony, don't. If you don't want to do a father-daughter dance, don't. If you want to wear a peach colored dress instead of a white one, go for it girl! Some of the best weddings are those that break with tradition and do something unique, especially if that unique factor showcases the couple's personalities and passions. Do whatever is *you* as a couple, no one else. Your grandma will get over it and may even appreciate your spunk!

Have a back-up plan. This is where having that wedding planner comes in handy. They are full of back-up plans and last-minute fixes for potential worst-case scenarios. What would you do if your hair and makeup artists showed up at the wrong hotel? What would you do if your officiant had a family emergency and couldn't make it to your ceremony? What would you do if your ceremony was supposed to be in your parents' backyard but it started thunder storming an hour beforehand? Make sure you work with all of your vendors to have a back-up plan in place for any unforeseen circumstances. The more prepared you are to handle such crazy, one-of-a-kind situations, the better.

CHAPTER 4
COMMON SENSE ON GUESTS

Guests come first. You've likely been a guest of at least one wedding. And if not, you've probably heard about enough bad wedding guest experiences from family and friends. So, what's the best way to ensure your guests are floored by how amazingly awesome and fun your wedding is? It's really quite simple: Take off your bride and groom hats, and put yourself in their shoes when planning the logistics of your day.

Most guests will tell you that what they remember the most about a particular wedding is the food/drinks and the music/dancing. Notice that invitations, décor, speeches, flowers, and bridal party attire are *not* some of the wedding highlights for guests. That's not to say that these items aren't important aspects of the entire wedding picture, but it's smart to keep them in perspective, especially if you have a limited budget. Excellent food, delicious drinks, and a lively dance floor will guarantee a memorable wedding experience for your guests. So don't stress if you decide to go with silk flowers instead of real ones. Few will notice and even less will remember or care.

If you're having an outdoor ceremony and reception in the Midwest in the dead of summer, it's probably going to be…no, it will be hot and humid. So, have some water and fans available for your guests. And, try to keep the ceremony short and sweet. You don't want your grandma to faint or your groom to sweat through his tan colored tux. Also, don't forget to ensure your venue has an air-conditioned space where guests can escape to should the heat get to them. The same goes for an indoor winter wedding, except with heating of course. A comfortable room temperature is critical to the comfort of your guests. So, make sure adequate heat and air-conditioning are available at your venue. I should also note that sufficient bathroom facilities for your number of guests are a must!

Remember, this is the first event that you and your spouse are hosting as a married couple. Do you want to be remembered as the wedding with cold chicken and a crappy amateur band where all of the guys sweat through their dress shirts? I think not!

Give your friends a plus one. In all honesty, it comes off as tacky, cheap, and could even be perceived as rude if you don't give your single adult friends the option to bring a date to your wedding. It's just not in good taste to only give people with a significant other a plus one. Giving your single friends the option to bring a date doesn't necessarily mean that they will bring someone, but it will make them feel more comfortable and it shows them that you respect them as a fellow adult. And, it's definitely not okay to fail to give an adult a plus one when you know that they're married or engaged. Common sense on that one, guys.

The same goes for adult family members who are single. When it comes to cousins for you 20 some year olds, a good rule of thumb is anyone your age or older should be given a plus one. Of course if your 20-year-old cousin has been dating the same girl for 6 years and she's practically part of the family, you can certainly make an exception and invite her. While the above are my suggestions, like all planning decisions, use your common sense to determine who should get a plus one.

Don't over-invite. Don't assume that certain guests you invite will "regretfully decline" your invitation. Although the rule of thumb says that 15-30% of your invite list won't be able to attend your wedding, you shouldn't bank on those percentages. You could be so thoroughly loved or have your wedding at the coolest place ever, that literally almost everyone says they can come. Well, if your venue only holds 250 people, and 280 of the 290 guests you've invited say they're coming, then you have a problem. So, avoid having a "Crap! What are we gonna do?" moment, and invite the number of guests your venue and your budget can accommodate.

Create a hotel block for your guests. Even if most of your guests are not from out of town, a hotel block near your venue is always a good idea. You should give your guests the option to stay at a hotel should they not want to drive after your reception. Let's be honest: Boozing is often part of the wedding celebration. Keep your guests safe by offering a hotel block. Even better, ask the hotel if they will offer a shuttle service for your guests to and from your reception site. This is often a free (yes, free!) service that hotels will provide when you reserve and fill a room block.

Still not sure about the perks of a hotel block? Consider this: Setting up a wedding hotel block often results in significantly reduced room rates for your guests. Meaning, they'll be charged much less than what they'd otherwise pay at the same hotel were they to fly solo when booking (aka without a block). Trust me when I say, your guests will love you for the negotiated room rate.

Offer your guests convenient parking options. While this can be tricky with city weddings, it's your responsibility as bride and groom to accommodate your guests with convenient parking options, preferably ones that don't cost an arm and a leg or require a mile long walk to your ceremony or reception site!

Keep your ceremony and reception close in time and distance. Having an 11:00 a.m. ceremony and a 6:00 p.m. reception, regardless of whether they're at the same or different locations, is not ideal for your guests, especially those that perhaps just drove in for the day and don't have a hotel room to hang out in for a few hours. It's best to keep your ceremony and cocktail hour start time within 3 hours of each other.

The same goes for distance: The shorter, the better. Don't make your guests drive from your hometown for the ceremony to a reception site that's more than 45 minutes away. Chances are many, if not most, of your guests will forgo the ceremony altogether and just go to the reception. To avoid this, try to keep your ceremony and reception sites within 30 minutes drive of each other. Also, be sure to give your guests clear directions to your ceremony and reception venues. Sometimes they'll need more than just an address if the location is difficult to find. An insert in your wedding invitation and a directions page on your wedding website are great communication tools to ensure that your guests know where they're going and how to get there.

"I can see the sucker, but I can't get to it." – *Eugene Sullivan*

Create a wedding website. Sound daunting? Don't worry, my friend. There are numerous online wedding planning websites that offer customizable tool kits to build your own wedding website absolutely free of charge!

Having a website is a great way to communicate all day-of logistics to your guests. You can post information about your ceremony and reception including locations, times, and requested attire. A wedding website also serves as a platform where your guests can get to know you as a couple before attending your wedding. You can have a page about how you met, how your proposal went down, and photos of the two of you throughout your relationship. We live in a digital age, so let your guests get to know you before your big day, and create a wedding website.

Play a variety of music. Chances are you're not inviting all 20 to 30 year olds to your wedding. And even if you were, it's doubtful they'd all have the same taste in music. Whether you hire a band or a DJ, make sure they're capable of playing a variety of music from different genres and eras. If you want guests of all ages on the dance floor, playing hip-hop all night long won't do the trick. Mixing in some oldies with some country, some rock and roll, and some new age hits will keep your dance floor rocking.

On a related note, don't be afraid to give your band or DJ a "Do Not Play" list. If you really don't want to hear certain songs on your wedding day, your band or DJ should know that beforehand. On the flipside, if you have songs that you want to hear, make sure you communicate those on a "Must Play" list before your wedding day.

Favors are so not necessary. The truth about favors is that most guests will a) forget them at the wedding, b) leave them in their car only to be thrown out 4 months later, or c) if they're edible, eat them on the car ride home and forget about them. Although they're a nice gesture, favors are not socially necessary. If you still feel like you *must* give your guests something to take away, consider a photo booth station. I can guarantee they'll remember that far more than some tiny pouch of personalized mints that cost you an unnecessary $500. Not to mention, a photo booth creates another fun experience for guests both young and old.

CHAPTER 5
COMMON SENSE ON ATTIRE AND BEAUTY

Order your dress early. The best rule of thumb is to order your bridal gown at least 8 months before your wedding day. Some designers take a number of months to custom make a wedding dress, and you want to have enough time to get your dress fitted and altered so it fits like a glove on your big day.

In a similar vein, order your bridesmaid dresses at least 5 months before your wedding. The best-case scenario is to have all of your girls order at the same time through the same boutique to guarantee that the dresses are from the same dye lot. This will ensure color consistency between your maids. Lilac from dye batch 1 could be entirely different from the shade of lilac from dye batch 10, even if the dresses are ordered from the same boutique and made in the same factory.

Order your dress in the right size. Don't order your dress 2 sizes smaller than your bridal consultant suggests. While you may have every intention of losing 20 pounds by the time your dress arrives, think of the nightmare it would be for your dress to arrive 6 weeks before your wedding day and you realize at your first fitting that you can't zip the back past your hips! Eek! Not a good situation for your seamstress, not to mention your self-esteem and your wallet.

Wear comfortable shoes. Okay, at least *bring* comfortable back-up shoes. I know you 5'2" brides want to be closer to your 6'2" man, but is breaking an ankle or tripping on your dress really worth the few extra inches of those stiletto heels? You'll likely be wearing a long dress and will maybe have a couple of photos taken of your shoes, but most of your guests won't even see them.

You're probably going to be wearing these suckers for over 10+ hours straight. You want to be able to move and groove with your man and your guests. The best advice is to avoid heels all together. But, realistically, most of you will want at least a little heel. Either way, make sure you have a pair of comfortable flats with your wedding planner or maid of honor. Don't start your Hawaiian honeymoon off with puss-filled blisters on your heels. Wear or bring flats, ladies.

"My dogs are barking." – Eugene Sullivan

Do not. I repeat, do not do your own hair and makeup. It's your wedding day. If you never pamper yourself another day in your life, do it on your wedding day. Don't add another stressor to the mix by leaving your beautification process to yourself. The $250 you invest in your hair and makeup will be well worth it when you don't have mascara running down your cheeks as you walk down the aisle or a bobbi pin pop loose and release a frizzed curl from the side of your head during pictures.

You want to look your very, very best on your wedding day and in the pictures you show to your children and grandchildren. Think about that before you opt to cut hair and makeup from your budget. Oh, and don't forget to do at least one trial with your hair stylist and makeup artist to avoid any beauty snafus on your big day. And while you're at it, go ahead and spring for that mani pedi girlfriend! You deserve to look and feel beautiful on your wedding day.

"You have to suffer to be beautiful." – Therese Sullivan

Have a wedding day survival kit. For any last minute touchups or a quick snack, it's important to have an emergency kit of sorts on your wedding day. You can keep it with your maid of honor or, better yet, with your wedding planner. Suggested emergency kit items follow on the next page.

WEDDING DAY SURVIVAL KIT

Baby powder

Bobbi pins

Bottle of water

Cash/checkbook
Just in case!

Clear nail polish

Concealer

Double sided tape

Extra earring backs

Eye drops

Floss

Lip gloss

Makeup remover

Meds
*Pain reliever, allergy med,
antacids*

Mini deodorant &
perfume

Mini first aid kit
*Band-Aids, liquid
bandages, antiseptic*

Mini hair spray

Mini lotion

Mini mirror

Mini sewing kit
*scissors, needles, thread,
buttons, safety pins*

Mini superglue

Mints

Phone charger

Q-tips

Snack
Granola bars, crackers

Stain remover pen

Straws

Tampons

Tissues

Tweezers

White chalk
*To cover up an wedding
dress imperfections*

CHAPTER 6
COMMON SENSE ON FOOD AND DRINK

There's nothing wrong with chicken just like there's nothing wrong with fish, or a buffet, or a family style meal, or food stations. Don't limit yourself by believing that only a grandiose steak plated meal with a top-shelf bar is appropriate for your wedding. You can save upwards of $20 per plate if you opt for chicken or fish. Multiply that by 150 guests and that's a savings of over $3,000. As long as you've selected a quality venue and have had a good tasting experience, there's no reason why you can't go with a less expensive food and drink option. Anyone who tells you otherwise can foot the bill!

Have a vegetarian and gluten-free option. We all know people are becoming more health conscious, and some of your guests may have real health issues that require them to eat a certain way. Be sure your venue is aware of any dietary restrictions that might exist. You may not know all of your guests' eating requirements, so, at the very least, have a vegetarian and gluten-free option available should someone request it.

Have an open bar. Think about it: If you're having alcohol at your wedding, your guests will be completely taken aback when then are asked to pay for their drinks. They've likely already paid to travel to your wedding and have gotten you a gift of some sort. Some are probably paying to stay at a hotel. Maybe they even took a day off from work to travel to your wedding. Needless to say, they've made sacrifices to be there to support you on your big day. The least you can do is give them a cold beer for free!

Oh, I should also mention, please, please, please have enough bar stations and bartenders for your number of guests. A good rule of thumb is 50 guests to 1 bartender and 150 guests to 1 bar station. Nothing will halt the dance party or sour the guest experience like a long bar line.

Serve appetizers. There is typically a long period between your ceremony and dinner. If you're having a cocktail hour, it's smart to offer some form of appetizers. They don't need to be excessive, but some bruschetta, meatballs, and cheese plates will be much appreciated by your hungry guests and should stave off your college friends from indulging in too many cocktails pre-dinner.

Serve a late-night snack. Like appetizers, a late-night snack is also a wise choice for a long reception. Your guests will be hungry after dancing all night and hitting up the bar. So, if it's in your budget, go ahead and indulge in those mini burritos, a hot dog station, or pizzas from your favorite local delivery spot. Just think of the possibilities! Add a personal touch and some flare to your late-night party with a snack to remember.

CHAPTER 7
COMMON SENSE ON BRIDAL PARTIES

Include your brothers and sisters. While you may be tempted to ask all of your girlfriends and best buds to be in your bridal party, consider your siblings first. Your siblings and your betrothed's siblings will likely be in your life for many, many years. And, even if you're not close now, adulthood and life's circumstances will likely draw you closer throughout the years to come. As the saying goes, friends will come and go, but family is forever.

Think it through before asking. Don't let your excitement get the better of you and ask 8 of your closest friends to be your bridesmaids the second after you get engaged. Give yourself and your fiancé some time to mull over the decision as to whom you'd like to stand by your side on your wedding day. A quick tip is to think about whom you envision being close with for years and years to come. There is no need to rush your bridal party decision.

Don't ask your bridesmaids to spend a fortune. Yes, your bridesmaids have made a commitment to stand by your side on your wedding day. This commitment comes with known costs including a dress, shoes, a bachelorette party, hair and makeup, and, perhaps, a shower. They know they'll have to cough up some cash to be part of the celebration, but don't abuse your bridal power.

Remain considerate of your maids and choose a dress and shoes that everyone can afford. A $500 bridesmaid dress and $200 pumps could create a huge financial burden for some, if not all, of your bridesmaids. The last thing you want is to create tension within your bridal party, especially tension directed at you! And, if you're really wanting that all-inclusive bachelorette party in Mexico, just be prepared that some of your maids and other invitees may not be able to afford the trip.

So, if you want your whole crew there and happy, opt for something more affordable. Oh, and I promise you, no one (not even your pictures) will know the difference between a $500 dress and a $200 one. So keep your bridesmaids content and be considerate of their expenses.

Don't do a joint bachelor/bachelorette party. If you do, it's neither. It's just another Saturday night of you and all of your friends hanging out and getting drunk. Enough said.

CHAPTER 8
COMMON SENSE ON CEREMONIES AND RECEPTIONS

Know your state's marriage license requirements. Each state is different in terms of license costs, certified documents you need to present, the waiting period from the time the marriage license is issued and the time the marriage ceremony is performed, criteria for witnesses to sign the marriage certificate, and other marriage license requirements and costs. State marriage license laws are also constantly changing, so be sure you're aware of your state's requirements and any recent changes in the months leading up to your wedding.

Have your groom and officiant mic'd up during your ceremony. Nothing is more frustrating as a guest than not being able to hear the officiant's message or the bride and groom recite their vows. It completely takes away from the ceremony experience. An easy fix is to set up a microphone for the officiant and clip another one to the groom's tux. Videographers can often provide this for you if your ceremony venue does not offer audiovisual services.

Plan for the weather. If you're planning a summer wedding, please don't make your bridesmaids wear heavy, boxy, nude colored, taffeta dresses. They'll not only have sweat stains in your photos; they could faint during pictures (and will probably look like pale, washed-out blobs in your photos); and they may not like you very much afterwards. Keep your bridal party comfortable and go with lightweight, flattering dresses and tuxes.

Planning an outdoor ceremony or reception? You best have a back-up plan. I promise you, Mother Nature won't care if it's your wedding day or not. If a blizzard in April is in the cards, you better have an indoor space in your back pocket.

"It's colder than a well digger's butt." – Eugene Sullivan

Choose wisely who gives speeches and toasts at your rehearsal dinner and reception. If your maid of honor or best man is painstakingly shy and utterly uncomfortable speaking in front of people, what kind of a sibling or friend are you if you force them to give a speech in front of 100+ people on such an important occasion as your wedding? Hint: Not a very good one.

No one likes to sit through an awful speech that

someone is struggling to get through. It's literally painful. A better alternative would be to have your maid of honor and best man tag team a speech together, or perhaps speak with another bridesmaid or groomsman. There is power (and confidence) in numbers! You can even have someone entirely different give a speech or a toast, or leave more time for dancing and forgo the speeches altogether.

On the flipside, if you know your best man or maid of honor will be half in the bag when giving their speech, or if you have a feeling they will get inappropriate in what they say, don't be afraid to talk to them beforehand and ask to take a look at their words of wisdom. Not being surprised about what they share with your guests is undoubtedly 100 times better than your grandma, let alone your new bride, hearing about how stoned you two got and how many people you made out with one night in college. And God forbid you have a videographer that gets it all on film!

It's also a good idea to keep speeches and toasts short and sweet. Three to five minutes is a good rule of thumb for speeches, and one minute for toasts. Don't bore your guests, and don't delay the food, dancing, and mingling!

"God bless." – Eugene Sullivan

Avoid over-the-top centerpieces and décor. Here is the blunt, honest truth: No one will remember or even care about your centerpieces. Shocking, I know. In fact, grandiose, large centerpieces, while beautiful, will obstruct your guests' view of the dance floor, those across the table from them, and, most importantly, of *you,* the bride and groom who they came to see! Guests don't want to be peering through an oversized vase of orchids to catch a glimpse of the wedding action. So why spend $3,000 on centerpieces? The answer is simple: Don't. When thinking about décor, just remember KISS (keep it simple stupid). Small vases and votives go a long way.

Don't leave too soon for your honeymoon. Enjoy your reception and celebrate to the very, very end with your family and friends. Remember, the day will go by fast, and you'll regret not spending as much time in the moment as possible. So, as tempting as it may be to book that red eye deal, refrain! Don't plan a late night or early morning flight the day of or after your wedding. Beyond the fact that you'll want to keep partying and soaking it all in at your reception until the wee hours of the night, you're going to be exhausted afterwards, not only from your wedding day, but from the months and months of preparation leading up to it. So, give yourself at least a day to recover and leave for your honeymoon a good 24-48 hours after your reception ends.

CHAPTER 9
COMMON SENSE ON BEING BRIDE AND GROOM

Take a break. Planning your wedding is a marathon, not a sprint. Honestly, planning a wedding in less than 6 months is a very tall order. So, don't rush through your planning process, and try to enjoy every step of the journey.

Eat. Eat. Eat. I cannot stress this enough. It's especially true for you, brides. You've probably yogaed, pilattied, ran, swam, lifted, and suffered through the no-carb, no-sugar diet for umpteen months leading up to your wedding so that you can fit into that beautiful dress and look fabulous next to your dashing husband. Am I right?

That's all well and good, but remember this: Your wedding dress will be heavy. Even if it's silk or lace, it will be heavier than anything you normally wear. This means that it will take effort and energy to wear it for more than 10+ hours straight. You don't want to faint on the altar, or feel lightheaded as you talk to your guests, or prove to everyone that a famished bride is a "hangry" bride. Eat before the ceremony, eat at your reception, and make sure you're not just hydrating with champagne all day.

Afraid you'll forget to eat? The day will be a whirlwind and it's easy to forget how long you've gone without so much as a cracker. Give your maid of honor, or another maid, or better yet, your wedding planner the task of feeding you throughout the day.

"My dinner bell is going off." – Eugene Sullivan

Spend some alone time as husband and wife on your wedding day. Whether you do a first look photo session or a solo limo ride to your reception, take at least 10-15 minutes on your wedding day to spend time alone as a couple. Cherish those moments together and take in the significance of the day with your new spouse.

Don't sweat the small stuff. Something will go wrong. You are human. Your wedding guests are human. Your wedding vendors are human. Humans make mistakes. Humans are not perfect. Your wedding day will not be perfect, but it will be absolutely incredible and unique to you as a couple. Oftentimes it's the "glitches," the little "oopsies" that make for life's best memories. The same is true for your wedding day.

So, don't sweat it if your bridesmaid picks an updo you wouldn't, or if your normally bubbly flower girl needs her mom to walk her down the aisle because she gets sudden stage fright, or if you forget your throw away garter on your dining room table. Hell, your best friend might even spill half of her glass of red wine on the front of your wedding dress right before your grand reception entrance (thank God for club soda and quick-thinking coordinators). Don't fret. The show will go on and you will be married! Remember, that's the most important thing. Oh, and don't worry if it storms; you can control nature even less than you can control humans. Plus, they say rain is good luck!

"If you fall, don't wait to rise." – Eugene Sullivan

ABOUT JACLYN TOOPES

Born and raised in the Northwest suburbs of Chicago, Illinois, I grew up with a deep-seated love for all things family, sports, planning, parties, and writing.

Getting married has been the best decision I've made in my life. The honest truth is that hanging out with your best friend day in and day out is a marvelously adventurous and joyous way to live life. I wouldn't have it any other way.

My husband, Ryan, and I own a Chicago-based wedding planning business, Toopes Events. And, we thoroughly enjoy each journey we're lucky enough to embark on with our clients as we help them plan a wedding celebration that is uniquely them.

I must say that I owe Ryan (he'll probably say I owe him a puppy) for his unwavering love and patience as I worked through getting my advice on paper in the hopes to make life just a little bit easier for future brides and grooms. Whether he gets that puppy or not, I'm truly grateful to have him as my rock.